Cover: Glentanner Station with the Ben Ohau Range as a backdrop. (Andris Apse)

Front endpapers: The sun setting on tussock farmland above the Timaru river in
  Hawea, Otago. (Andris Apse)

Previous page: Bright green farmland in Wanaka, Otago. (Andris Apse)

Opposite: The bush-clad hills of Westland as the clouds roll in. (Andris Apse)

Overleaf: Wild flowers decorate this farm north of Kawakawa. (Focus New Zealand, Brian Moorhead)

ISBN 1-86958-191-1

© 1995 Hodder Moa Beckett Publishers Limited

Published in 1995 by Hodder Moa Beckett Publishers Limited
[a member of the Hodder Headline Group]
28 Poland Rd, Glenfield, Auckland, New Zealand

Printed through Bookbuilders, Hong Kong

BACK COUNTRY

NEW ZEALAND

Hodder Moa Beckett

THE BACK COUNTRY reflects the diversity of landscapes in New Zealand and the challenges that face the large country stations and the people who farm them. Against backdrops of snow-capped mountains, wild rivers and expansive plains, sheep and cattle are mustered and crops are harvested.

The panoramic images selected here capture the breathtaking rural and coastal scenes that typify New Zealand back country from the far North to central Otago. It is a memorable record of the countryside that makes New Zealand such a unique and special place to live in and visit.

Black cattle against bright green pastures, hillsides dotted with white sheep, herds of soulful-eyed deer are all memories which are captured here, reflecting the dramatic landscapes in all four seasons.

Enjoy the stunning panoramas through the eyes of some of New Zealand's best photographers and marvel at the rugged and awe-inspiring back country.

Sunrise on farmland at the head of the
Whangaroa Harbour, Northland. (Andris Apse)

Overleaf: The golden hues of a dry summer,
north of Houhora. (Focus NZ — Brian Moorhead)

Corrugated-iron architecture typical of the New Zealand barn. (Fotopacific, Westpics)

Overleaf: Undulating green hills in the shadow of Mt Taranaki. (Fotopacific)

In the centre of the North Island, Ruapehu is a spectacular backdrop for grazing sheep.

(Focus NZ, Brian Moorhead)

A villa is an elegant homestead on the Hauraki Plains.

(Fotopacific, Alan McConie)

Hay in storage for the winter. (Fotopacific)

Bright green grass is a striking backdrop to the cattle of Erewhon Station in Taihape. (Andris Apse)

Musterers and dogs from Braemar Station in the Mackenzie country, with the Southern Alps behind. (Andris Apse)

Overleaf: Sheep clamber over the tussock of Braemar Station. (Andris Apse)

Some stations offer tourist activities, such as
horse-trekking on Glentanner Station. (Andris Apse)

Mt Cook from Glentanner Station. (Andris Apse)

Sheep being herded along the back-country roads are a common sight in New Zealand. (Andris Apse)

Overleaf: Rolls of hay are a dramatic foreground feature of the golden plains of the Mackenzie country. (Fotopacific, Mark Walsh)

A cattle muster near the head of Lake Ohau,
Mackenzie Country. (Andris Apse)

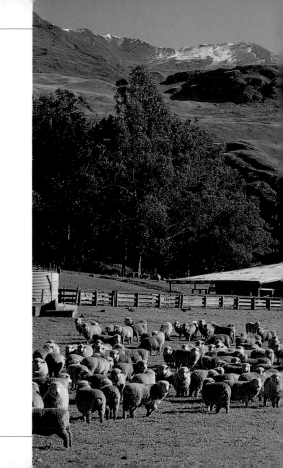

Glendhu Bay Station beneath snow-capped mountains, Lake Wanaka, Otago. (Andris Apse)

Sightseeing down the rugged Ahuriri Valley, Otago.

(Andris Apse)

The head of Lake Tekapo in spectacular colour. (Andris Apse)

Sheep feed on hay as winter reaches Ben Aron Station, Ahuriri Valley, Otago. (Andris Apse)

Overleaf: Sheep muster at Dunstan Downs Station, Otago. (Andris Apse)

Walter Peak Station homestead on the shores of
Lake Wakatipu. (Andris Apse)

Previous Page: Sunlight catches the hills of Glenorchy, Otago. (Andris Apse)

An autumn vista in the Matukituki Valley, Otago.
(Andris Apse)

Deer graze near Queenstown, Otago. (Andris Apse)

Back endpapers: **Rolling green farmland in South Canterbury, near Fairlie.** (Andris Apse)